European History for Kids

Vol. 1

A Captivating Guide to the Early History of Europe from Prehistoric Times, through Ancient Europe and the Middle Ages, to the Renaissance and the Age of Discovery

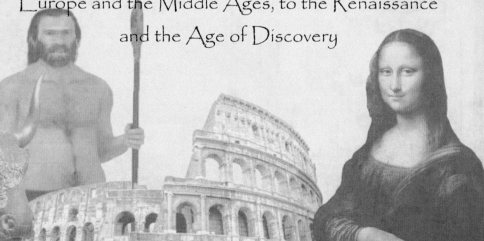

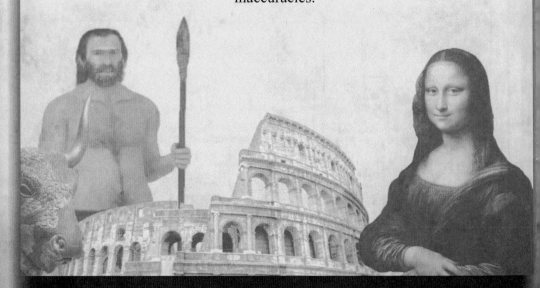

Table of Contents

Introduction   1

Chapter 1: The First Europeans   2

Chapter 2: The Bronze Age and the Iron Age   11

Chapter 3: Ancient Europe   21

Chapter 4: The Middle Ages   35

Chapter 5: Renaissance   50

Chapter 6: The Age of Discovery   60

Conclusion   68

If you want to learn more about tons of other
exciting historical periods, check out our other books!   69

References   70

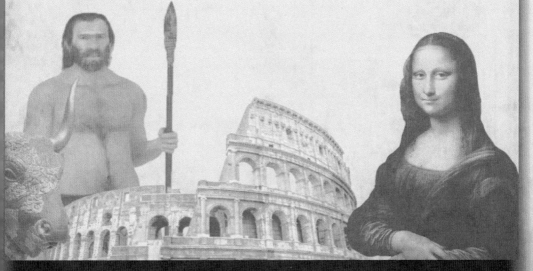

INTRODUCTION

Europe is the second smallest of the seven continents we split the earth into. As of today, Europe is made up of forty-four countries and is in the *Northern Hemisphere*. The Northern Hemisphere is the half of the earth north of the *equator* (an imaginary line that runs through the middle of the earth halfway between the North and South Poles).

Fun Fact: Europe only covers approximately two percent of the earth!

In this book, you will explore the vast history of this continent. Starting in *prehistoric* times when the first *Homo sapiens* appeared in Europe, you'll go through the age of *antiquity*, into the *Dark Ages*, and end your quest with the *Renaissance* and the *Age of Discovery* when Europe once again flourished and new worlds were explored. You will gain valuable insights into what life was like throughout Europe, how it has developed through time, and the impact its history has had on the rest of the world.

History will come alive as you whizz through thousands of years of fascinating stories, achievements, and unbelievable events. To make learning enjoyable and engaging, this book contains fun facts, interesting activities, and insightful images throughout. So, without further ado, let's journey back to the first stop on your adventure through time—when cavemen ruled the earth!

Chapter 1: The First Europeans

Before the first European *Homo sapiens* (*ho-mo-say-pee-uhnz*), the name for the species of modern-day humans, there were *Neanderthals* (*nee-an-der-talls*) in Europe. Neanderthals were a type of prehistoric man and a near relative to Homo sapiens. Based on fossil and genetic evidence, scientists think Neanderthals evolved from another type of subhuman species somewhere between three and seven hundred thousand years ago.

A reconstruction of what a Neanderthal man may have looked like.

Early Homo sapiens appeared in Europe during the *Stone Age*. It is called this because people began using stone tools during this time. The Stone Age is made up of three periods: *Paleolithic* (*pay-lee-uh-li-thuck*), *Mesolithic* (*meh-zuh-li-thuck*), and *Neolithic* (*nee-uh-li-thuck*).

The first Homo sapiens to appear in Europe were the *Cro-Magnon* (*krow-mag-non*). The remains of these first Europeans were found in 1868 in France, but more remains have been discovered throughout Europe. The Cro-Magnon people were around during the Paleolithic period (also known as the *Early Stone Age*) from c. 40,000 to c. 10,000 years ago.

Unlike the Neanderthals before them who had slanted foreheads, the Cro-Magnon had straight foreheads, wide faces, and big chins. Their brains were a little larger than ours are today, but they had similar bodies and could speak. At five foot five or so on average, the Cro-Magnons were taller than other early humans.

The Cro-Magnon people were mostly *nomadic* or seminomadic. This meant they did not farm and stay in one place but moved around, following the animals they were hunting. Like the other cavemen before them, they were hunter-gatherers. They hunted large animals like woolly mammoths, bears, horses, or reindeer and gathered plants, berries, nuts, and seeds to eat. The Cro-Magnon hunted using spears they made from antlers, bone, and a type of rock called *flint*. The Cro-Magnons created statues and cave paintings. They also spun *flax* fibers to sew clothing and make rope and baskets. Because of their nomadic lifestyle, they lived in caves or built shelters from rocks, tree branches, and animal fur.

A reconstruction of an early Cro-Magnon man.

Around 10,000 BCE, the previously nomadic people underwent the *Neolithic (nee-oh-li-thuck) Revolution* and started to form settlements. This first started in the Middle East in *Mesopotamia (meh-so-puh-tay-mee-uh)*, and by 7,000 BCE, Greece and some other parts of southeastern Europe also began to farm. People began introducing agriculture: instead of hunting and gathering food, they grew plants and bred livestock. This is why the Neolithic Revolution is also called the *Agricultural Revolution*.

Fun Fact: This period of history is known as the Neolithic or New Stone Age.

While historians cannot be sure what caused the Neolithic Period to begin, it could have been the climate, which began to get warmer following the last *ice age*. An ice age happens when the temperature of the Earth's surface and atmosphere drops, and the ice caps and glaciers expand, taking up most of the planet. Once the ice had begun to melt and the planet got warmer, the land was more fertile and easier to cultivate. Scientists also believe that the human brain may have advanced and that people became intelligent enough to discover agriculture.

Fun Fact: Ice ages can last millions of years! The last ice age was about 2.5 million years ago and lasted until about 11,700 years ago.

Map of the Late Neolithic Period in Europe.
Joostik, CC BY-SA 3.0 <https://creativecommons.org/licenses/by-sa/3.0>,
via Wikimedia Commons, https://commons.wikimedia.org/w/index.php?curid=22961869

The Agricultural Revolution did not happen at the same time throughout Europe, though. Some places like England and Scandinavia didn't start to farm until thousands of years later. The first farmers in Greece and southeast Europe seem to have cultivated plants similar to those of the people in the Middle East, while other areas of Europe began *domesticating* animals before farming crops. Domesticated animals are pets or livestock that have been tamed. Before this, all animals were wild.

Evidence suggests that Europe could have been the first place where many types of animals were domesticated. The first place horses were domesticated was Ukraine, and people in other parts of Europe also domesticated cows and pigs.

Fun Fact: Early Europeans were the first to domesticate dogs, and they began doing this before the Agricultural Revolution during the Mesolithic period. So, we have them to thank for man's best friend!

It is thought that dogs descended from wolves in Europe. The wolves would approach the nomadic people living there for scraps of food. Less aggressive wolves would succeed in getting food, so they were the ones that survived. Man and wolf developed a mutually-beneficial relationship, as wolves were useful for hunting. Over time, the wolves evolved into dogs through a process known as *selective breeding*. The most loyal and tame wolves would be bred so that each new litter would be a little more domesticated. The close relationship between humans and dogs has led to them becoming our beloved pets today.

Once the people of Europe were no longer nomadic, they began to build more permanent homes. Some of the most well-preserved examples of Neolithic dwellings can be found in *Skara Brae (skaa-ruh-bray)* in Scotland. The houses were made from stone and contained furniture, pottery, tools, and jewelry.

Prehistoric European Jewelry.
By Gary Todd from Xinzheng, China, CC0, via Wikimedia Commons,
https://commons.wikimedia.org/w/index.php?curid=101200684

Fun Fact: The Stonehenge monument in England was built during the Neolithic Period. It is one of the greatest mysteries of all time, as no one knows how or why it was built.

A photo of Stonehenge.

Chapter 1 Challenge Activity

1. Who were Europe's first people?

2. What was the Agricultural Revolution?

3. What age were the Paleolithic, Mesolithic, and Neolithic periods part of?

4. What does the word "nomadic" mean?

5. What process was used to turn wolves into dogs?

1. Who were Europe's first people?

   The Cro-Magnon

2. What was the Agricultural Revolution?

   The Agricultural/Neolithic Revolution was when people began living in settlements, farming, and domesticating animals.

3. What age were the Paleolithic, Mesolithic, and Neolithic periods part of?

   The Stone Age.

4. What does the word "nomadic" mean?

   It means that people would move around hunting and gathering and did not live in one place.

5. What process was used to turn wolves into dogs?

   Selective breeding.

Chapter 2: The Bronze Age and the Iron Age

Following the Stone Age, mankind entered the period known as the *Bronze Age.* Like the Stone Age before it, the Bronze Age earned its name because people began using bronze to make tools, weapons, and art. Bronze is an *alloy* made from melting metals together—mostly copper, a small percentage of tin, and sometimes other metals. When it cools, the result is bronze. Previously, people had started to use copper. However, when bronze was discovered (perhaps by accident), they realized it was stronger and therefore a sturdier choice for their weapons and tools.

As with the Agricultural Revolution, all of Europe did not enter the Bronze Age at the same time. By 3000 BCE, the Bronze Age had started in Greece, but it didn't reach Great Britain until 1900 BCE.

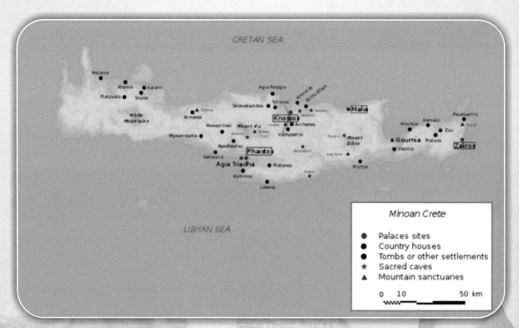

A map of Minoan Crete.

When bronze was first discovered, only the rich could afford it. But, over time, it became more affordable and helped civilizations to expand and develop. During the Bronze Age, the wheel and the ox-drawn plow were invented, which further aided in the growth of civilization.

The first advanced civilization of Europe during the Bronze Age was the *Minoans*. The Minoan people lived on the island of Crete and its surrounding islands in the *Aegean (ah-gee-uhn) Sea*.

While Minoan civilization began much earlier, it flourished between 2000-1500 BCE. The Minoans became powerful through trading with the Greek mainland and nearby Cyprus, Egypt, and Syria. Their main exports were olive oil, timber, and wine, which they would trade for metals and jewels. Their capital city was called *Knossos (no-sos)*. In the center of the city, there was a big palace filled with artwork and pottery.

Fun Fact: According to Greek mythology, there was a gigantic labyrinth (la-buh-rinth, a type of maze) under the palace in Knossos where a monster called a Minotaur (mi-nuh-toor) lived. The Minotaur had the body of a man and the head of a bull.

Bulls had special significance in Minoan culture and were featured heavily in their pottery and artwork. Bulls were symbolic of power and strength. In one Greek legend, the hero *Hercules (her-kyew-leez)* had to defeat the *Cretan Bull* that was terrorizing the people of Crete as part of his *Twelve Labors*.

Minoan bull's head c.1500 BCE, found in Crete.

By Jebulon - Own work, CC0, https://commons.wikimedia.org/w/index.php?curid=39669128

However, the Minoans were not the first advanced European civilization. Many other civilizations in Europe developed around the same time. One society that started shortly after the Minoans (yet peaked and ended earlier) was *Los Millares* in Spain, which flourished between 2700 and 2400 BCE. The people of Los Millares could have been descendants of the Minoans, or they at least came into contact with them and were influenced by them. We know this because their *necropolises* (*nuh-kro-puh-luhs*, burial grounds) were built in the same style as the early Minoans.

Los Millares itself was a copper mining settlement and home to around one thousand people. The city was surrounded by walls and had a fort to defend the people and the valuable copper inside. Los Millares had a strong economy and would trade with its neighbors.

Around 2300 BCE, Central Europe entered the Bronze Age. This period is known as the *Unetice (yew-nuh-tis) culture* and was made up of communities throughout Central Europe. Within the Unetice culture there were also the *Straubingen, Adlerberg* and *Hatvan* cultures.

Fun Fact: The countries that make up Central Europe are Germany, the Czech Republic, Poland, Slovenia, Slovakia, Hungary, and Austria.

Perhaps the most famous artifact discovered from the Bronze Age in Germany is the *Nebra sky disk*. Historians believe that the Nebra sky disk is the oldest example of an accurate map of the universe.

The Nebra Sky Disk.

They think it may have been used to plan for harvest. Only fifteen miles away from Nebra, the remains of Europe's oldest observatory, *the Goseck Circle*, were discovered. Nicknamed "Germany's Stonehenge," these remains provide further evidence that the people of this time had some knowledge of outer space and the cosmos.

Another notable Bronze Age civilization in Europe is the *Mycenaean (mai-suh-nee-uhn) civilization*, which followed the Minoan civilization. The Mycenaean civilization flourished in the Late Bronze Age (1700-1100 BCE). The Mycenaean people lived on mainland Greece and are known as "the first Greeks" because they were the first to develop

A map of Europe during the late Bronze Age.

the Greek language. They were named after their biggest city, *Mycenae*. In addition to Mycenae, Greece had many other city-states, including *Athens (a-thuns)* and *Thebes (theebz)*. Around 1450 BCE, the Mycenaeans conquered the weakening Minoans. They took over their islands and adopted much of their culture. Like the Minoans before them, the Mycenaeans traded with neighboring civilizations.

After the Bronze Age, the next period of humanity is called the Iron Age. The people of this age transitioned to using iron to make weapons and tools instead of bronze. Toward the end of the Late Bronze Age and the start of the Early Iron Age, a civilization known as the *Hallstatt culture* began to flourish in Austria.

The introduction of iron *smelting* (the process of applying heat to metal ore to get the base metal) during this time directly impacted Hallstatt culture. Its people could now make stronger tools, farming equipment, and weapons. Because their settlement had many natural iron deposits, iron was useful for trading. The area also had an abundance of salt to mine and trade with.

The Hallstatt culture is sometimes referred to as *Proto-Celtic (pro-toe-keltic)* because of its similarities to another culture of the time, the ancient *Celts (kelts)*. The Celts consisted of many different tribes that lived in Western and Central Europe, but certain tribes traveled even further. The Celtic tribes shared a language and similarities in religion, culture, and warfare.

Iron Age Celtic weapons.
By Gary Todd from Xinzheng, China - Iron Age Europe Celtic Weapons, CC0,
https://commons.wikimedia.org/w/index.php?curid=101201865

Fun Fact: Many Celtic tribes were lost during the Roman Empire. However, some Celtic people remained in Great Britain. Celtic languages are still spoken in remote parts of Scotland, Ireland (both Gaelic), and Wales (Cymru). A Celtic language called Breton is also still spoken in Brittany, France.

The Celtic religion was *polytheistic*, meaning it had several gods. The Celts' religion highly valued nature, so many areas of land, natural rivers, and springs were considered sacred. The religious leaders were called *druids (droo-uhds)*, and they were greatly-respected, high-ranking people. They would also act as teachers and judges. Druids did not want to leave behind written records, even though they could write. There are a few possible reasons for this. They may have believed words lost their power when they were written down, that people would no longer memorize things and it would be harmful to their memory, or they did not want to share their knowledge.

Celtic artwork is recognized for its geometric patterns, swirls, and knots. The Celtic knot has several different styles. The basic premise of the Celtic knot is that its design has no start or end. Because of this, it is believed that the knots represent eternity.

An example of one type of Celtic knot.
By Nevit Dilmen, CC BY-SA 3.0 <http://creativecommons.org/licenses/by-sa/3.0/>,
via Wikimedia Commons, https://commons.wikimedia.org/wiki/File:Celtic_knot_red_nevit.png

The final noteworthy European Iron Age civilization is the *Etruscan (uh-truh-skn) civilization*, Italy's first great civilization. Before the Etruscan civilization was the *Villanovan culture*, which started around 1100 BCE and had become Etruscan by approximately 750 BCE. Etruscan civilization consisted of independent city-states that shared a common culture, language, and religion.

The Etruscans were polytheistic. In addition to having their own gods, they also adopted some deities and heroes from nearby Greece, the most famous being Hercules. When the Etruscans eventually fell under the Roman Empire, much of their language and culture was lost. However, the Romans chose to adopt many Greek gods and myths, so Hercules became one of their deities, too.

Chapter 2 Challenge Activity

Can you place the below Bronze and Iron Age civilizations in order within the three time periods?

Bronze Age

Late Bronze Age/Early Iron Age

Iron Age

Etruscan civilization

Mycenaean Greece

Minoan civilization

Los Millares culture

Hallstatt and Celtic cultures

Unetice culture

Bronze Age

Minoan civilization

Los Millares culture

Unetice culture

Late Bronze Age/Early Iron Age

Mycenaean civilization

Hallstatt and Celtic cultures

Iron Age

Etruscan civilization

Chapter 3: Ancient Europe

Now that you are an expert on *prehistoric Europe* (before 800 BCE), we will discover the main cultures of *classical antiquity* in Europe (the ancient past before the Middle Ages) between 800 BCE and 500 CE.

ANCIENT GREECE

The first important civilization to emerge in classical antiquity was Ancient Greece. Historians divide ancient Greek history into three periods.

The Archaic Period

The Archaic period began in 800 BCE when, following the end of the Mycenaeans and the Dark Ages, ancient Greek civilization emerged. During the Archaic period, Greece consisted of about one hundred city-states. The two main cities were Athens and *Sparta*.

A map of Greece at the start of the Peloponnesian Wars

The people of Athens were interested in the arts and learning, while Spartans were known for being great warriors. The two cities were often at odds and would later go on to fight each other in the Peloponnesian (peh-luh-pol-nee-shun) Wars.

During this time, many advancements were made throughout Greece, and several have impacted life as we know it now. Many great works of literature were written in the Archaic period, including the two famous epic poems by Homer: the *Odyssey* and the *Iliad*. These poems tell mythological stories that involve many great Greek gods, heroes, and monsters.

The Greeks were polytheistic. The twelve primary Greek gods were called the *Olympiads* and lived on *Mount Olympus*. The chief god was called *Zeus* (zyoos); he was the god of the sky and ruler of all gods and men. His weapons were lightning bolts and thunder. His brother, *Hades* (hay-deez), was the ruler of the underworld where the dead lived. His other brother, *Poseidon* (puh-sai-dn), was the god of the sea and carried a *trident* (a spear with three points). There were many more gods and lots of goddesses. Two Greek goddesses were *Aphrodite* (a-fruh-dai-tee), the goddess of beauty and love, and *Athena* (uh-thee-nuh), the goddess of war and wisdom.

Greek mythology also followed many great heroes who would defeat monsters, often with the help of the gods. Perhaps the most famous Greek hero was *Hercules* (hur-kyuh-leez), a *demigod* (half-man, half-god) who famously completed twelve labors. Some examples of Greek monsters are three-headed dogs, giants, dragons, *cyclopes* (one-eye creatures), and *Medusa*, a *Gorgon* with snakes for hair who would turn you to stone if you looked at her!

Fun Fact: Theater was also invented in this period by a man called Thespis. The two styles of Greek theater were tragedy and comedy.

In addition to watching actors in plays, the Greeks also loved to watch sports. The famous Olympic Games were invented in the Archaic period. Originally, the games took place in *Olympia* every four years. Some ancient Olympic sports are still played in today's games: boxing, wrestling, the javelin and discus throw, and the long jump. Luckily, today's wrestlers no longer have to fight naked like back then!

Fun Fact: Pythagoras (pi-tha-guh-ruhs), the inventor of the Pythagorean theorem for geometry, was born during this period. His theory is still taught in math classes today.

Law and order improved during this time. *Draconian laws* (named after their creator, Draco) were introduced. These were very strict, and many offenses were punishable by death. This is why we often refer to out-of-date or harsh laws as "draconian."

Democracy was also established in the Archaic period. This meant Greece would be run by a government of elected officials who wrote their own constitution.

The Archaic period ended with the second Persian invasion of the *Greco-Persian Wars*, in which the Persians tried to conquer Greece. Despite being heavily outnumbered in battle often, the Greek armies emerged victoriously.

A depiction of a Greek soldier (carrying a shield with the mythical flying horse, Pegasus) fighting a Persian.

https://commons.wikimedia.org/w/index.php?curid=5507148

The Classical Period

The next era of Ancient Greece is known as the *Classical period.* This is the main time we think of when discussing Ancient Greece. During this period, Greece made great advancements in philosophy. One of the leading philosophers of the Classical period was a man called *Socrates (so-kruh-teez).* His *Socratic method* was the basis for modern Western philosophy, which is why he is nicknamed "The Father of Western Philosophy."

Toward the end of this period, Greece was conquered by *Alexander the Great*. He was able to unite all of the city-states under one ruler. He also founded the Greek Empire, which included parts of Europe, Asia, and Egypt. In Egypt, he created the new city of *Alexandria*. After this, Greek pharaohs ruled Egypt. They refused to adopt Egyptian ways and ran Alexandria as a Greek city. The Classical period ended with Alexander the Great's death in 323 BCE.

The Hellenistic Period

The final period of Ancient Greece is known as the *Hellenistic period*. During this time, Greece began to decline until it eventually fell to the Romans in 146 BCE. The Hellenistic period ended in 31 BCE when the last Greek city, Alexandria, finally fell to the Romans.

Theda Bara as Cleopatra and Fritz Leiber as Caesar in the 1917 movie Cleopatra.
https://commons.wikimedia.org/w/index.php?curid=6072136

THE ROMAN EMPIRE

The next most important ancient European civilization was the Roman Empire. Ancient Rome started when the capital city of Rome was founded in 753 BCE. In the beginning, Rome was ruled by kings, but in 509 BCE, the king was replaced with an elected government called the *Roman Republic*. The Republic introduced many laws and a constitution. Like the Greeks, this style of government would go on to influence modern-day democracy. During this time, Rome began to expand into new territories throughout Italy and the Mediterranean. The Romans would later conquer Spain, Sicily, Turkey, Greece, and Macedonia.

The most famous Roman slave was *Spartacus* (*spaa-tuh-kuhs*), who escaped and led an army of slaves. When he was enslaved, Spartacus had to fight as a *gladiator* (*gla-dee-ay-tuh*). Gladiators were professional fighters who fought in *colosseums* (large *amphitheaters*—a type of open-air circular arena) for people's entertainment. Because the fights would often end in death, most gladiators were slaves or criminals. However, some men would become gladiators for the glory: it was seen as glamorous, and many gladiators became famous. Gladiators were so popular that women would swoon over them and children would play with action figures of them. It wasn't just men who fought —some women even became gladiators!

The Colosseum/Flavian Amphitheater in Rome.
Diliff, CC BY-SA 2.5 <https://creativecommons.org/licenses/by-sa/2.5>,
via Wikimedia Commons, https://commons.wikimedia.org/w/index.php?curid=2127844

Rome ceased to be a republic in 45 BCE when Julius Caesar took control and declared himself dictator for life. His rule did not last long, though, as he was assassinated just one year later. However, this did not restore the republic as his assassins hoped. His son, *Octavian (ohk-tay-vee-uhn)*, became the first emperor of Rome in 27 BCE. He then changed his name to *Augustus Caesar* and began the Roman Empire.

Rome continued to expand its empire until its peak in 117 CE. Throughout their empire, the Romans built roads, bridges, and *aqueducts (ah-kwa-duckts)*, man-made channels that transported water to the cities.

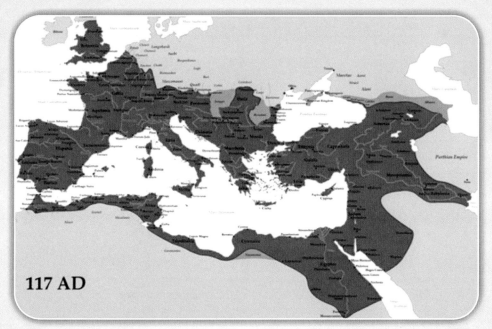

A map of the Roman Empire at its peak.
Tataryn, CC BY-SA 3.0 <https://creativecommons.org/licenses/by-sa/3.0>,
via Wikimedia Commons https://commons.wikimedia.org/w/index.php?curid=19625326

Initially, the Romans were polytheistic and adopted many of the Greek gods. All the planets in our solar system (apart from Earth) are named after Roman gods. Jupiter was similar to Zeus, Neptune was based on Poseidon, and Mars was based on the Greek god of war, Ares. They were also named after goddesses such as Venus, who was similar to the Greek Aphrodite.

In 312 CE, the emperor *Constantine (kon-stuhn-teen)* converted to Christianity, and eventually, the religion spread throughout the Roman Empire. Many countries that the Romans introduced Christianity to are still Christian today. It is interesting to note that the Romans adopted Christianity, as they had persecuted the Christians and Jews for hundreds of years. In fact, it was the Romans in Palestine who sentenced Jesus to death by crucifixion in 29 CE.

The Romans left many legacies that impact our world today, from roads and buildings that still stand to the spread of Christianity and democracy. They have also influenced the languages spoken throughout Europe. The Romans spoke Latin, which is the basis for modern-day French, Spanish, Portuguese, and Italian. Many English words also have roots in Latin.

Fun Fact: Roman numerals (numbers) are still used today—for example, in the Super Bowl or when naming kings and queens.

Roman Baths in Bath, England.

THE GOTHS/BARBARIANS

Today the words "goth" and "barbarian" have very different meanings from ancient times. The Goths were a group of people who flourished towards the end of antiquity into the start of the Middle Ages. It is unclear where they originated, but they may have been from Scandinavia. The Goths were made up of two groups, the *Visigoths* and the *Ostrogoths*.

Fun Fact: The word barbarian originally meant "foreign invader" in Greek.

The Goths were often referred to as barbarians because they were indeed foreign invaders. The Visigoths are perhaps most famously known for *the Sack of Rome*. They were the first people to defeat the city of Rome in more than eight hundred years! The

A painting of the Sack of Rome.
https://commons.wikimedia.org/w/index.php?curid=3905581

word "barbarian" was often used negatively, as people believed they were destroying Roman art and culture. However, this was not strictly true: they absorbed some Roman cultural customs, created Roman-influenced art, and adopted Catholicism.

After this, the Visigoths moved to *Gaul* (modern-day France and parts of other bordering countries) and *Iberia* (the peninsula made up of Spain, Portugal, and Gibraltar). The Visigoths eventually lost France to the *Franks* and later lost Iberia during the Muslim invasion.

The Ostrogoths settled where modern-day Ukraine is now located. They were eventually defeated by the *Huns* and joined *Attila the Hun* (the leader of the Huns) and his army. Once the Huns fell, the Ostrogoths set their sights on Italy. This led to years of fighting with the Italians. While the Ostrogoths were initially successful, they eventually lost.

Fun Fact: The word Goth (goth) has gone on to have many different meanings. In the Middle Ages, the word gothic referred to a type of architecture. Then, in the 18th and 19th centuries, gothic referred to a type of literary fiction. The most famous gothic writings of this time are perhaps Frankenstein by Mary Shelley, Dracula by Bram Stoker, and the works of Edgar Allen Poe. Today, the term goth is used for a particular style and cultural group. Generally, people who identify as goths often wear lots of black clothing and white makeup and listen to heavy metal music.

Actor Boris Karloff as Frankenstein's monster in the 1931 movie Frankenstein.

Chapter 3 Challenge Activity

1. Who fought in the Peloponnesian Wars?

   A) Athens and Rome

   B) Greece and Persia

   C) Rome and the Visigoths

2. Who was the Greek god of the sea?

   A) Zeus

   B) Poseidon

   C) Hercules

3. What did the Romans adopt from Greece?

   A) Their clothing

   B) Their weapons

   C) Their gods

4. Who ended the Roman Republic?

   A) Julius Caesar

   B) Alexander the Great

   C) Emperor Constantine

5. What are the Visigoths most famous for?

   A) Their architecture

   B) The Sack of Rome

   C) Joining Atilla the Hun

Chapter 3 Answer

1. Who fought in the Peloponnesian Wars?

    A)   Athens and Rome

    B)   Greece and Persia

    C)   Rome and the Visigoths

2. Who was the Greek god of the sea?

    A)   Zeus

    B)   Poseidon

    C)   Hercules

3. What did the Romans adopt from Greece?

    A)   Their clothing

    B)   Their weapons

    C)   Their gods

4. Who ended the Roman Republic?

    A)   Julius Caesar

    B)   Alexander the Great

    C)   Emperor Constantine

5. What are the Visigoths most famous for?

    A)   Their architecture

    B)   The Sack of Rome

    C)   Joining Atilla the Hun

Chapter 4: The Middle Ages

The Middle Ages, also known as *medieval times*, span the thousand years between 500 and 1500 CE. The fall of the Roman Empire was the main catalyst for the transition from antiquity to the Middle Ages. Near the end of European antiquity, the once-powerful Roman Empire began to crumble. Eventually, it split into two empires: East and West. When Rome fell to the Goths, the Western Roman Empire weakened further and ultimately fell just before the start of the Middle Ages. After this, the *Dark Ages* in Europe began, and the Eastern Roman Empire continued as the *Byzantine Empire* until 1453 CE.

Fun Fact: The period following the collapse of Rome at the start of the Middle Ages is referred to as the Dark Ages because there was no longer a central government keeping records. This means historians know less about this time than they did when the Romans were in power. (The Romans were excellent record keepers.)

THE FRANKS

The first notable people of the Middle Ages in Europe were the Franks. They originated in Northern Europe and moved down to Gaul. When Gaul later became called France, it was named after the Franks. During the Middle Ages, the Franks had two distinct *dynasties* (ruling families). The first was the *Merovingian (meh-ro-vin-g-uhn) dynasty* (509-751 CE), followed by the *Carolingian (ka-ro-lin-g-uhn) dynasty* (751-843 CE).

The first Merovingian king, *King Clovis*, united the Franks, and they defeated the Goths under his rule. When he converted to

Christianity, he was the first ruler to be recognized by the pope as King of the Franks. The most successful Frank ruler was also part of the Carolingian dynasty. Under *King Charlemagne (shar-luh-mayn)*, the Franks expanded their empire through most of Europe. He was also appointed the first *Holy Roman Emperor* by the pope. This meant he was considered to be the leader of all European kings.

A map of Europe in 814 CE following the death of Charlemagne.

https://commons.wikimedia.org/w/index.php?curid=23527053

The main contributions that the Franks provided to medieval times were two concepts: the *feudal system* and knights. Under the feudal system, all land was distributed to knights and lords. When a knight died, his sons would inherit not only his land but also his knighthood. Being a knight wasn't cheap—the horses they rode and the armor they wore were costly, so only the wealthy could become knights. Land would usually be given to knights if they were brave in battle or in return for their sworn loyalty and sword to fight for the king.

An artist's rendition of a medieval knight on horseback.

Sebacalka, CC BY-SA 4.0 <https://creativecommons.org/licenses/by-sa/4.0>, via Wikimedia Commons, https://commons.wikimedia.org/w/index.php?curid=55613195

ANGLO-SAXONS

At the start of the Middle Ages, a group called the *Anglo-Saxons* (*an-glow sack-sons*) managed to invade Great Britain and were the dominant people of England from 550 to 1066 CE. The Anglo-Saxons consisted of three groups of German-speaking people from Germany, Denmark, and the Netherlands: the *Angles*, *Saxons*, and *Jutes*.

The Angles settled the areas of Northumbria, Mercia, and East Anglia to the north. The Jutes settled on the southeast coast of Kent, while the Saxons had Sussex and Essex in the southeast and Wessex in the southwest.

The Anglo-Saxons had a *hierarchical* society with a king at the top. Beneath the king were bishops and noblemen known as *thanes*. They would advise the king and help him rule. A group of these advisors was called a *witan*. Regular people were known as *churls*, and at the very bottom were slaves. Slaves were either prisoners of war or people who could not pay their debts, and they had no rights.

A painting of Beowulf and his men carrying Grendel's head.
https://commons.wikimedia.org/w/index.php?curid=11001844

THE VIKINGS

Another Germanic group to settle in Great Britain in medieval times was the *Vikings*. The Vikings were *Norsemen* (Northmen) that originally started in Scandinavia before expanding into Britain, Germany, and Iceland. They later expanded into northeastern Europe and France, where they formed Normandy. The Vikings greatly influenced medieval Europe, especially during the *Viking Age* between 800 and 1066 CE.

The Vikings were ruthless invaders who would sail to other parts of Europe in longships and raid villages. They had a bad reputation and were often called barbarians because of their lack of remorse over attacking defenseless *monasteries* (mo-nuh-stair-eez—religious buildings where medieval monks lived) and stealing from them.

Fun Fact: The word Viking meant "to raid" in the Old Norse language.

The Vikings were polytheistic, and you might be surprised to learn that you're already familiar with some Old Norse gods thanks to the Marvel superhero movies! Their primary god was *Odin*, the god of war. Odin was depicted as an old man with only one eye, as he had given up the other in exchange for wisdom. Odin's son, *Thor*, was the god of thunder and wielded a hammer. *Loki* was the trickster god who was adopted by Odin and could shapeshift.

Fun Fact: Vikings who died in battle were heroes and would go to Valhalla, the Viking heaven, where they would feast on a banquet with the gods. This belief helped the Vikings to be extremely brave in battle, as this was the only way they would end up in Valhalla.

Viking longships are one of the more iconic things we think of when we hear the word Viking. The boats were long and thin with curved ends and had a sail and oars to steer with. They were ideal for use in shallow water so the Vikings could land on beaches. The ships were not only important to the Vikings for raiding trips, but they also played a part in their burials. High-ranking people would be buried or cremated in their boats. The boat would be pushed out into the water and then set on fire.

A Viking funeral at sea.

THE NORMAN CONQUEST

You have probably noticed the date 1066 coming up quite a lot in this chapter, and that's no coincidence! This was the year of the *Norman Conquest*, when the Normans defeated England. The Normans were Vikings who came from Normandy in France. That year, the King of England, *King Edward*, died without leaving an heir to the throne. Unfortunately, three men believed they were the rightful heir to the throne. They were *King Harald Hardrada of Norway*, *Earl Harold Godwinson of England*, and *Duke William of Normandy.*

Fun Fact: William of Normandy is now more often called William the Conqueror.

Immediately after King Edward died, Earl Harold crowned himself king. However, the other two potential kings weren't going to give up the throne that easily! King Hardrada was the first to invade England to try to claim the crown. But he ultimately lost to Harold and was killed in battle. Only a few days later, the Normans invaded. On October 14, 1066, the English army fought against the Norman army in the *Battle of Hastings.*

Although the armies were equally matched in size, the English army was tired from having just fought another battle. The Normans had more archers and a bigger cavalry (soldiers on horseback). This gave the Normans the upper hand, and they finally won when an arrow killed Harold. The English continued to resist, but eventually, the English nobles accepted they had lost and crowned William the King of England on Christmas Day.

A scene from the Bayeux Tapestry.
https://commons.wikimedia.org/w/index.php?curid=25609093

THE CRUSADES

The Crusades (krew-sayds) were a series of holy wars between European Christians and Muslims in which the *Holy Roman Empire* tried to take control of the Holy Land, Jerusalem. Jerusalem was important to many religions during this time. The Christians wanted it because it was where Jesus was crucified and resurrected. The

Muslims wanted it because it was the site of Muhammed's ascension to heaven. And the Jews wanted it because it was where King Solomon built the first temple for God.

Although Jerusalem had been Arab-occupied for many years, it was taken over by the *Seljuk Turks* in 1070 CE. Unlike their predecessors, the Seljuk Turks did not allow the Christians to pilgrimage there. Because of this, the Byzantine Emperor and the pope amassed an army to try to take back the Holy Land, and the wars began in 1095 CE.

Fun Fact: There were ten crusades that spanned two hundred years, one of which was run by children! An army of thousands of children marched off, but mysteriously, none of them ever made it to the Holy Land—and many did not return home.

The first crusade was the most successful, as the European army of 300,000 men took control of Jerusalem. Unfortunately, they lost control again in the following wars and never managed to regain it. However, following the third crusade, Christian pilgrims were again permitted into the Holy Land.

As you might expect, the Christian army consisted of knights. But peasants and common folk were also enlisted. Many people joined the cause because they believed it would help them get into heaven or would allow them to earn their fortune. The symbol of the holy crusaders was a red cross. This would be proudly displayed on their clothing, flags, and standards.

Fun Fact: The famous Knights Templar were formed during the Crusades. They had a reputation for being fervently devout, brutal fighters and were forbidden from retreating unless they were hugely outnumbered.

A drawing of the Knights Templar and Crusaders.
https://commons.wikimedia.org/w/index.php?curid=18457521

THE HUNDRED YEARS' WAR

The Norman Conquest wasn't the only fight to take place between England and France in the Middle Ages. In 1337 CE, the Hundred Years' War between the two countries began. The war was a series of small battles between bouts of peace. The wars started because the King of England claimed he was the rightful heir to the French throne. After this, the two countries continued to fight over many things.

Although it is called the Hundred Years' War, it actually lasted longer, taking place from 1337 to 1453 CE.

Perhaps the most famous military leader of the Hundred Years' War is *Joan of Arc*. Joan was a French peasant girl who, at just twelve years old, had a vision in which she was visited by the Archangel Michael. The angel told her that she must lead the French in a battle against the English. However, it wasn't until she was sixteen that she finally fulfilled her visions. With Joan's faith rallying the troops, she successfully defeated the British in many battles. Eventually, in 1431 CE, Joan was captured by the English and burned at the stake. She was only nineteen years old.

Because the British could not prove Joan was a religious heretic, the flimsy excuse they found for sentencing her to death was that she had worn men's clothing!

A painting of Joan of Arc.
https://commons.wikimedia.org/w/index.php?curid=100589506

THE BLACK DEATH

It wasn't just wars that killed lots of people during the Middle Ages. There was also a plague known as the *Black Death* that ravaged Europe between 1347 and 1350 CE. The disease, believed to be the *bubonic (bew-bon-ik) plague*, was highly contagious, and there was no cure if you caught it—around sixty percent of those who got it died.

Fun Fact: It is thought that the plague was called the Black Death because sufferers would get blue and black bruise-like splotches all over their bodies. The disease was so awful that it killed at least a third of all people in Europe in just three years. In fact, it killed anywhere between seventy-five and two hundred million people! So many people died each day that it was impossible to properly bury them and the dead had to be thrown in huge pits.

Fun Fact: The economic impact of losing so many people was massive, and it is estimated to have taken one hundred and fifty years for Europe to recover.

The bubonic plague was transmitted by fleas living on rats and is thought to have arrived in Europe on the rats aboard trading ships from Asia. It was such a deadly disease that many people would die within twelve hours to one week of being bitten by an infected flea. Unfortunately, the people at the time did not know that rats and fleas were to blame. Instead, they thought it was God punishing them. Many cities were very dirty and filled with thousands of flea-ridden rats, so the plague spread quickly and easily, sometimes wiping out entire populations.

Understandably, medieval people were terrified of the Black Death, especially when they found that staying inside and burning the dead—or entire cities—did nothing to slow the disease. Scientists are unsure how the plague ended, but it is thought that quarantines helped. Over the years, the bubonic plague has reappeared, but it has never been as severe or killed as many as it did during the Black Death.

Chapter 4 Challenge Activity

1. What is the period of European history extending from c. 500 to 1500 called?

2. What event marked the end of European antiquity and the beginning of the Middle Ages?

3. What are the Angles, Saxons, and Jutes also known as?

4. Who believed in the Old Norse gods (Odin, Thor, Loki, etc.)?

5. What year did the Norman Conquest and Battle of Hastings take place?

6. What holy war were the Knights Templar formed during?

7. Which famous heroine was reportedly visited by the Archangel Michael?

8. Which two creatures helped to spread the bubonic plague/Black Death?

Chapter 4 Answer

1. What is the period of European history extending from c. 500 to 1500 called? The Middle Ages or medieval period.

2. What event marked the end of European antiquity and the beginning of the Middle Ages? The collapse of the Roman Empire.

3. What are the Angles, Saxons, and Jutes also known as? The Anglo-Saxons.

4. Who believed in the Old Norse gods (Odin, Thor, Loki, etc.)? The Vikings.

5. What year did the Norman Conquest and Battle of Hastings take place? 1066 CE.

6. What holy war were the Knights Templar formed during? The Crusades.

7. Which famous heroine was reportedly visited by the Archangel Michael? Joan of Arc.

8. Which two creatures helped to spread the bubonic plague/Black Death? Rats and fleas.

Chapter 5: Renaissance

Toward the end of the Middle Ages and the start of the early modern period (between the 14th to 17th centuries), there was a cultural movement throughout Europe called the *Renaissance (ruh-nuh-sons)*. The Renaissance was a movement that greatly improved and changed European intellectual life. It was a period of cultural and economic "rebirth" that promoted the rediscovery of classical art, literature, science, and philosophy. The Renaissance began in Florence, Italy, and spread throughout Europe.

A photo of Florence today.

Fun Fact: An important contributor to the Renaissance was a movement known as humanism. It promoted the rediscovery of classical work. The movement also claimed it was okay to want to pursue wealth and beauty.

The Renaissance likely began in Italy because of the legacy of the Roman Empire and the fact that the country had become very wealthy. This meant that people had the luxury to pursue their interests and could afford to support artists and scientists.

The Renaissance can be split into four main periods. These are called the *Proto-Renaissance* (1300-1400 CE), *Early Renaissance* (1400-1495 CE), *High Renaissance* (1495-1527 CE), and *Late Renaissance* or *Mannerism* (1527-1600). There were so many significant events and achievements during the Renaissance that it would be impossible to discuss them all in just one chapter. So, we will briefly mention the main achievements and people of this time.

PROTO-RENAISSANCE

This period took place just before the start of the Renaissance and laid the foundation for the movement. Artists such as *Giotto* paved the way for the realism movement within art during this period. Famous writers of this period include *Dante*, who wrote the epic poem *Divine Comedy*. One of the first humanists, *Francesco Petrarca* (also known as *Petrarch*), was named Rome's *poet laureate* (an officially appointed poet for government or royalty).

EARLY RENAISSANCE

During this time, many new leaders came into power, and the Byzantine Empire finally fell under the *Ottoman Empire*. In 1469 CE, *Lorenzo de Medici* became the ruler of the Florentine Republic. This was vital for the Renaissance, as Medici was a big supporter and used his power to spread the movement.

In 1450 CE, the German Johannes Gutenberg (yo-han-es goo-ten-burg) invented the printing press. This is considered the most important invention of modern times. Before this, it was impossible to write books on a mass scale, which meant few people could read. Thanks to this invention, literacy was improved, and the Renaissance and Scientific Revolution were able to happen.

Gutenberg-style printing press from the 17th century, exhibited at the Museu d'Art de Girona.

HIGH RENAISSANCE

The High Renaissance is considered the peak of European artwork, and many of the world's most famous works of art were created during this period.

An ideal that developed during this time was to be a "Renaissance Man" who could do it all.

The ultimate Renaissance Man was *Leonardo da Vinci (lee-uh-nar-doh da vin-chee)*. He was a talented artist who could paint and sculpt; he was also a scientist, inventor, engineer, architect, and writer. Da Vinci is considered one of the greatest artists of all time, yet only fifteen of his paintings still exist. Perhaps his most famous works of art are the *Mona Lisa* and *The Last Supper.*

Some people say that the Mona Lisa's eyes look like they follow you around the room!

Da Vinci was also interested in *anatomy*—a biological science that looks at the body structure of living things. In addition to drawing the human body, from muscles and organs to the skeleton, he also studied the anatomy of many animals. His journals contain over thirteen thousand pages containing ideas for inventions and buildings!

The Mona Lisa by Leonardo da Vinci.
https://commons.wikimedia.org/w/index.php?curid=15442524

Fun Fact: Leonardo da Vinci was the first person to study how man could fly—he even drew plans for a flying machine! Some people also think he may have invented the bicycle.

Another famous Italian Renaissance Man was *Michelangelo* (*mai-kuhl-an-juh-low*). He too was a talented painter and sculptor. His most famous works of art are his statue of *David* and his mural on the ceiling of the *Sistine Chapel*. He was also an architect and worked on many significant Renaissance buildings, including the *St. Peter's Basilica* in Rome. On top of this, he was also a poet who wrote three hundred poems!

Fun Fact: Leonardo da Vinci and Michelangelo became rivals after Michelangelo teased da Vinci for not completing a sculpture!

Fun Fact: The popular comic book, cartoon, and film characters known as the Teenage Mutant Ninja Turtles are named after four Italian Renaissance artists: Leonardo da Vinci, Michelangelo, Raphael, and Donatello.

LATE RENAISSANCE/MANNERISM

During this period, many significant events happened in Europe. Perhaps the most significant was the separation of the Church of England and the Catholic Church of Rome in England in 1534 CE. *King Henry VIII* created a new *Protestant* church, the Church of England, which was not under the pope's control. His main motivation for doing this was to be able to divorce his wife *Catherine of Aragon* and marry a new woman, *Anne Boleyn*. (At the time, the Catholic Church forbade divorce.) This led to unrest throughout Europe for many years and caused numerous fights between the Protestants and Catholics.

Portraits of Henry VIII and Anne Boleyn.
Dancingtudorqueen, CC BY-SA 4.0 <https://creativecommons.org/licenses/by-sa/4.0>,
via Wikimedia Commons, https://commons.wikimedia.org/w/index.php?curid=111570074

Other notable improvements in science also took place. A Polish man named *Nicolaus Copernicus (nick-oh-las koh-pur-nuh-kus)*, who studied math and astronomy, came up with the idea that the sun was at the center of the universe and that Earth revolved around the sun—not the other way around. At the time, many people did not agree with his theory, and it took almost one hundred years for his *heliocentric (heh-lee-oh-centrick)* way of thinking to be widely accepted.

Yet another Italian man who made an impact during the Renaissance was *Galileo Galilei* (gah-luh-lay-oh gah-luh-lay-e). He was a scientist, astronomer, and mathematician. His most famous achievements were improving the telescope, discovering the moons of Jupiter, and laying the foundation for the *scientific method*. Most Renaissance scientists studied classical works but didn't test them to see if they were true. However, Galileo decided to test the theories in the real world to see if he could observe them. Many people were angry with this because they didn't want the old ways to be questioned.

Last but not least, another important man who contributed to literature and theater during the Renaissance was the British playwright *William Shakespeare*. Shakespeare is considered one of the greatest writers of all time and wrote many famous plays that are still enjoyed and studied today. Shakespeare is credited with writing at least thirty-seven plays! His most popular works are *Romeo and Juliet*, *Macbeth*, and *Hamlet*. Like many other Renaissance artists, Shakespeare was influenced by Roman and Greek literature and mythology.

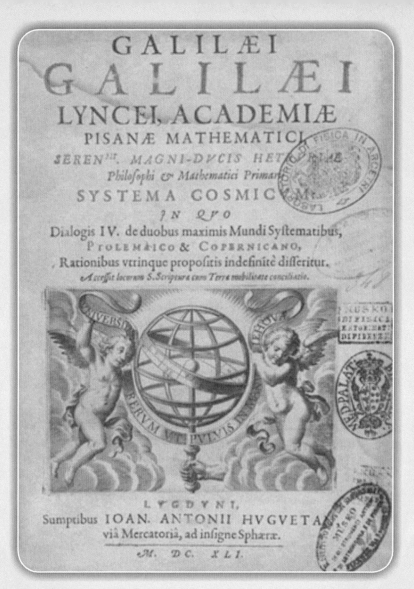

The front cover of The Dialogue Concerning the Two Chief World Systems.

Fun Fact: Shakespeare is credited with inventing and introducing over 1,700 English words that are still used today! He is nearly the single-most quoted writer—only the Bible is quoted more often than his works.

Chapter 5 Challenge Activity

Can you spot which statements are True or False?

1. The Renaissance was a cultural movement that greatly improved and changed European intellectual life.

2. One important event during the Renaissance was the fall of the Roman Empire.

3. The invention of a new printing press technology revolutionized European literacy.

4. Copernicus and Galileo both believed that the sun was the center of the universe.

5. Lorenzo de Medici and Leonardo da Vinci were the kings of England and France.

6. The Renaissance started in London, England.

7. King Henry VIII of England separated the Church of England from the Catholic Church so he could divorce his wife.

Chapter 5 Answer

True or False?

1. The Renaissance was a cultural movement that greatly improved and changed European intellectual life. True.

2. One important event during the Renaissance was the fall of the Roman Empire. False. The fall of the Roman Empire marks the start of the Middle Ages. However, the remaining Byzantine Empire (Eastern Roman Empire) did fall during this time.

3. The invention of a new printing press technology revolutionized European literacy. True.

4. Copernicus and Galileo both believed that the sun was the center of the universe. True.

5. Lorenzo de Medici and Leonardo da Vinci were the kings of England and France. False. Lorenzo de Medici was the head of Florence, Italy, and Leonardo da Vinci was a Renaissance artist and inventor.

6. The Renaissance started in London, England. False. It started in Florence, Italy.

7. King Henry VIII of England separated the Church of England from the Catholic Church so he could divorce his wife. True.

Chapter 6: The Age of Discovery

During the Renaissance, another important period in European history was taking place from the 15th to the 17th century. The Age of Discovery, also known as the *Age of Exploration*, was a time when Europeans began exploring the rest of the world. They discovered new routes and lands in India, the Far East, and the Americas. It was an important time for geographic discovery, as much of the previously-unknown world was mapped in a short time. To help the explorers with their voyages, they made advancements in navigation and mapping.

The main reason for the expeditions was to expand trade. After the Ottoman Empire captured *Constantinople* (modern-day Istanbul, Turkey), it shut down many trade routes between Europe, India, and the *Orient* (the countries in the Far East, including China). The wealth those trade routes had previously provided was no longer available, so the Europeans needed to find new routes to these places or other countries to trade with. The Europeans were especially interested in finding new places to trade for gold, silver, and spices.

The expeditions were incredibly dangerous, and many ships never returned. However, people still went on them seeking their fortunes. Some of the explorers were lucky and became very rich by discovering new places with a wealth of gold and silver or fertile land on which to establish new colonies.

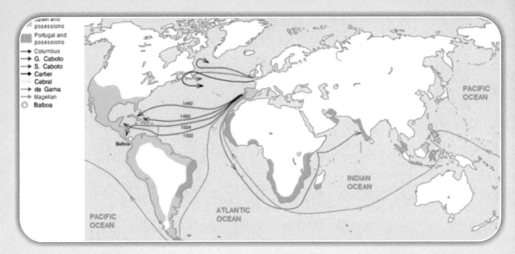

A map of the main journeys during the Age of Discovery.

The first expedition of the Age of Exploration was led by the Portuguese and a man called *Henry the Navigator*. They explored the west coast of Africa, traveling further south than ever before. A Portuguese sailor, *Bartolomeu Dias*, was the first European to travel beyond the southern tip of Africa and into the Indian Ocean.

Not wanting to miss out, the Spanish decided they, too, should explore in search of new trade. They were approached by an explorer named *Christopher Columbus*, who planned to sail west over the Atlantic Ocean. He believed this would take him to China, as the Europeans did not yet know that the Americas existed.

So, in August 1492 CE, Columbus and his men set sail in three small ships. Eventually, they landed on the Caribbean island of Barbados. However, Columbus mistakenly believed he had landed in the *Eastern Hemisphere* (lands to the east called the *East Indies*), so he began referring to the native people as Indians.

Fun Fact: It is because of Columbus' mistake that Native Americans are often referred to as Indians.

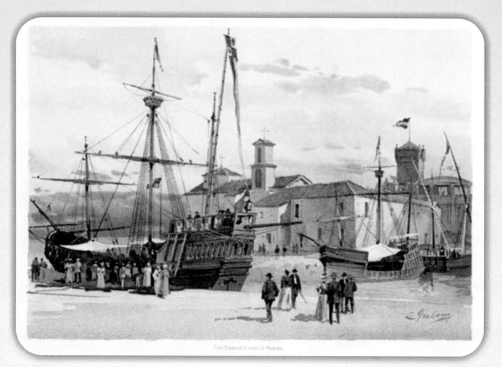

A painting of Columbus' three ships.
The Field Museum Library, No restrictions, via Wikimedia Commons
https://commons.wikimedia.org/w/index.php?curid=38155054

The Western Hemisphere (lands to the west), especially the Americas, was referred to as the New World.

Eventually, the explorers realized they had in fact discovered the Americas, and further expeditions were sent to explore the rest of the New World. It is worth noting that although Columbus is credited with "discovering" the Americas, this isn't strictly true. There were already many native people living in the Americas, and Europeans had already visited in 1000 CE. The voyage, led by a Viking called *Leif Erikson*, landed in Canada. However, that trip was not well recorded and did not impact European knowledge of the continent. Columbus is credited with its discovery because he was the reason Europe finally knew about the Americas and began to explore and colonize them.

Despite having made four voyages there, Christopher Columbus died without ever realizing that he had discovered the New World—he still believed he had found a shortcut to the Indies!

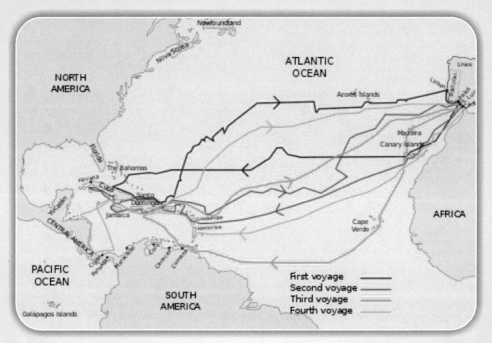

The routes of the four voyages Christopher Columbus made to the Americas between 1492 and 1503.

The two main countries leading the Age of Exploration were Spain and Portugal. It was decided in the *Treaty of Tordesillas* that they would split the New World equally. Spain was given the majority of the Americas, and Portugal got Brazil, India, and Asia. Later, Great Britain and the Netherlands also established colonies in the New World.

A map of Portuguese discoveries between 1415 and 1543.

Fun Fact: Great Britain went on to have the largest empire in history. Today, Great Britain only has a few overseas territories, but its monarch, Queen Elizabeth II, is the head of state for fourteen countries, including many Caribbean islands, Canada, Australia, and New Zealand.

After the main period of the Age of Discovery, expeditions to unexplored lands continued. In 1642 CE, Dutch explorer *Abel Tasman* landed in New Zealand. However, he somehow overlooked the giant country nearby, Australia! Following this, in 1770 CE, *Captain James Cook* of Britain also went to New Zealand and then discovered Australia. Like Columbus, he is credited with its discovery despite it being already inhabited by natives.

Many inventions and advancements during the Age of Exploration made these voyages possible. The magnetic compass and rose greatly helped explorers navigate the open ocean, as they reliably pointed to the magnetic north. Another navigational tool invented during this time was the *traverse board*, enabling sailors to record the speed and direction they were traveling to ensure they stayed on course.

Finally, important advancements were also made to ships themselves. The Portuguese designed a sailboat called a *caravel*. Caravels were important as they were cheap to build, small, and easy to maneuver. Plus, they could travel quickly and *windward*, or toward the wind.

A painting of a caravel.

Can you match the words/phrases below with their partners?

The New World	Toward the wind
Traverse Board	The term used to describe the Western Hemisphere (especially the Americas)
Caravel	A navigational tool that records the speed and direction of a ship
Windward	An explorer who discovered the Americas
Christopher Columbus	An agreement between Spain and Portugal to split the New World
Treaty of Tordesillas	A type of sailboat
The East Indies	An explorer who discovered Australia
Captain James Cook	The name for the countries in the Eastern Hemisphere during the Age of Discovery

Chapter 6 Answer

The New World	The term used to describe the Western Hemisphere (especially the Americas)
Traverse Board	A navigational tool that records the speed and direction of a ship
Caravel	A type of sailboat
Windward	Toward the wind
Christopher Columbus	An explorer who discovered the Americas
Treaty of Tordesillas	An agreement between Spain and Portugal to split the New World
The East Indies	The name for the countries in the Eastern Hemisphere during the Age of Discovery
Captain James Cook	An explorer who discovered Australia

Conclusion

Following the Age of Discovery, Europe entered a more disruptive and tumultuous time of many revolutions, the Great Depression, and two world wars. If you'd like to learn about this time, check out our book on Modern European History for Kids.

If you've enjoyed this book and would like to expand your knowledge on any of the times discussed, check out our range of Captivating History for Kids. We have plenty of books on Early European Civilizations and more to come! We also highly recommend the below resources for further reading and viewing.

If you want to learn more about tons of other exciting historical periods, check out our other books!

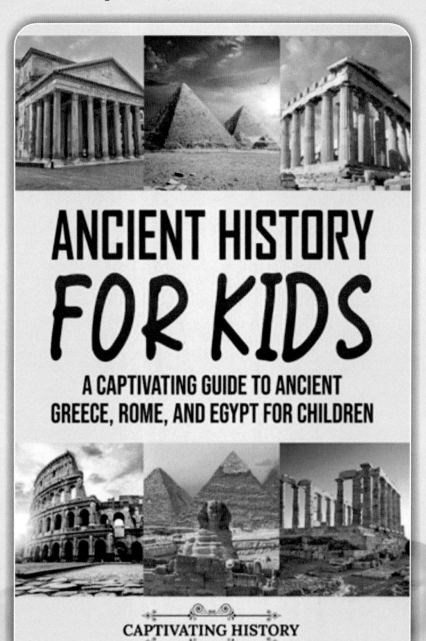

ANCIENT HISTORY
FOR KIDS

A CAPTIVATING GUIDE TO ANCIENT GREECE, ROME, AND EGYPT FOR CHILDREN

CAPTIVATING HISTORY

Click here to check out this book!

References

Websites

www.natgeokids.com

www.kids.britannica.com

Books

Horrible Histories - available on Amazon and major book retailers

Simple History - available on Amazon or at

https://simplehistory.co.uk/books/

YouTube Channels

Simple History https://www.youtube.com/c/Simplehistory

Crash Course https://www.youtube.com/c/crashcourse

TED-Ed https://www.youtube.com/teded